Giants of the Dawnland

Ancient Wabanaki Tales

Collected by Alice Mead,
Arnold Neptune and James Neptune

Loose Cannon Press
South Portland, Maine
Revised Edition, © 2015

This collection is dedicated
to the preservation of traditions,
culture and spirituality of the
Wabanaki Native People.

July 15, 2015

The project was supervised by
Arnold Neptune, Lieutenant Governor of the
Penobscot Nation.
The revised edition was supervised by James Neptune.

A portion of the sales from this book will go to the
Penobscot Nation Museum, Indian Island, Maine.

Cover Photo: Michael O'Hara

Table of Contents

Introduction: Dawn   viii

Part 1: Early Tales

1. Gluskape and the Wind Bird   1

2. He Who Was Unborn   4

3. Gluskape, the Giant Killer, and the Whales 10

4. The Loon Woman   22

5. The Chenoo's Icy Heart   14

6. Gluskape and the Mighty Wasis   31

7. The Magic Giants   34

Part 2: People and Animals

8. How Gluskape Found Summer   42

9. The Thunders and Mosquito Person   44

10. How Mahtigwess the Rabbit Became Wise   47

11. The Man Who Sang for Animals   52

12. The Partridge's Canoe   56

13. How the Micmacs Found Plants to Grow   58

14. Weasel Sisters Marry the Star People   61

Part 3: Stories of the People

15. A Boy Named Fox Fire   67

16. Gluskape and Turtle Person   70

17. The Orphan and the Mikumwess   75

18. The Girl Who Married Katahdin   79

19. Gluskape Leaves The Dawnland

          Epilogue: Dusk   82

History of the Dawnland Region

Geographically, the Wabanaki people were the four easternmost tribes in North America, the first tribes to see the sunrise. Since post-glacial times, these people lived– and continue to live– in Maine, New Hampshire, New Brunswick, Nova Scotia, and Newfoundland.

Rivers were the Wabanaki highways. For thousands of years, the people stayed along the seashores during the summer and moved north into the woods for the winter. In spring, during the melting of snow, they followed the rivers back to the sea.

Glaciers had once covered what is now Maine until 16,000 years ago. Frozen snow and seawater created masses of ice one mile thick. Then, the climate changed. After 3,000 years of melting, ponds, streams and rivers far bigger than they are today drained from the glaciers and flooded the Penobscot River Valley all the way up to Millinocket, Maine.

Slowly, with the weight of the glaciers receding, the rocky coast of Maine began to rise until it looked like it does today. With the leading edge of the glacier still in Canada, Maine was a tundra, covered not with trees but with moss, lichen, and shrubs. When the climate grew still warmer, trees grew. This was the time when the first people came to Maine. So did animals.

Twelve thousand years ago, large bears, giant beavers, bison, and elk all roamed the Maine wilderness. Many kinds of whales including killer whales swam in the Bay of Fundy and the Gulf of Maine. The Wabanaki lived by hunting and fishing, but greatly feared the long winters. The following stories date back to the earliest times of the people in this region, thousands of years ago. The tales filled people with knowledge and respect for their world, and there were literally hundreds of these stories. Without the information in these tales, the Wabanaki could not have survived for as long as they have. The stories told the Wabanaki people many things. Some are creation stories about why partridges live under bushes, or how whales spout vapor. Some are funny, like the story of the Mosquito Person, or the one about the Weasel sisters tricking the Wolverine to give him a nasty temper. Many stories tell the people how to treat others – not to be jealous, to be generous, patient, brave, and respectful, and to share what you have. Some tell about how to quiet crying babies, how to arrange a marriage, how to bury the dead. Others give important survival information. If you fear becoming lost in the fog, take a dog in your canoe that can sniff for land and point you home.

The stories tell about the history of the glaciers, how to avoid starvation, the songs of whales, where to build your winter camp, the value of persistence and foresight, and later the redemptive power of inner strength, music and songs. Originally, the stories were all songs; they were full of rhyme, puns, and rhythm. Today, for the most part, this musicality has been lost. The Wabanaki language itself communicates on many levels, describing how things live or appear so that others will be aware of these same attributes. Wabanaki people gave descriptive names to places so that others could find them. For example, Casco means the muddy place; Penobscot means the wide-open, rocky, river place.

The Concept of M'teouin

Central to all the stories is the concept of personal power –M'teouin. This is personal power and self-awareness that develops over time as a person matures. In the Dawnland, each person is an individual who must discover the source of his or her power himself. Without it, a family's survival is at stake.

Power can be found in many ways, in many places, but it takes perseverance, dedication and a long time to develop. Power can be found in an alliance with an old woman or orphan, a magical mikumwess, a gentle giant, a serpent's horn, in a chipmunk's skin, or among the poor and outcast. Imitating others or showing off will not bring power, nor will acting in envy, as the magic rabbit found out. People and animals can change shape, assuming and sharing in the power of others – teaching the people that nothing is as it seems on the surface.

Sadly, some stories tell of the end of Gluskape's time and the coming of white people to the Dawnland, of how the animals turned away from the People and no longer spoke the same language, how the forests, animal skins, and Native beliefs were lost to the dominance of the English, Scottish, and French colonists. By the 1600's, the people who had thrived there for nearly 12,000 years had nearly died out.

Some Wabanaki Storytellers: From 1882

1. Tomah Joseph – Passamaquoddy, Governor at Peter Dana Point Reservation

2. Marie Saksis – Penobscot, Old Town, Maine

3. Lucy Pictou – Nova Scotia, 1923

4. Louis Mitchell – Member of Maine Legislature, 1884

5. Louis Brooks

6. Sapiel Selmo – translator of Wampum Records

7. Noel Neptune – Penobscot, Old Town, Maine

8. John Gabriel – Passamaquoddy, Pleasant Point, Maine

9. Isabelle Googoo Morris – Nova Scotia, 1923

Prologue: Dawn

As if still in a dream, Gluskape rose from sleeping. Morning light reached through the trees and touched the lakes. He stood. Pine trees dripped from his arms and grew rooted in the ground. His long strides formed ponds as his snowshoes made dents in the spring-soft snow. He left behind ridges of hardwood – ash, birch, maple, as he strode across the Dawnland, eastward. Little animals, squirrels, turtles, and chipmunks trotted after him. His faithful loons were by his side, one named Loon and one named Wolf.

All day, Gluskape shaped the land, hollowing out ponds, pushing up ridges, carving rivers, and clearing streams. At night, he grew tired. As he stepped across the Bay of Fundy, islands like little rocky canoes scattered beneath his feet as he headed home. There, Grandmother Woodchuck tended his campfire. Gluskape settled down for the night. The evening sky, red between the black trees, meant it would be very cold. He slept but only a little, for the Dawnland was not yet rid of the evil faints who roamed the dark woods or the magic serpents that hid beneath the ground.

Strange things could happen to the people if they ventured too deep into the woods to hunt. There, facing the giants, the people would have to draw on their own power – their fierce bravery, careful preparedness, and their knowledge of the woods and the spirit world. Then they would be filled with m'teouin or power. One foolish, prideful decision could cost a life when alone and deep in the woods.

Gluskape and the Wind Bird:

(Passamaquoddy, told by Louis Mitchell 1884)

In olden times, far to the north, sitting on a rock at the edge of the sky lived a giant wind-bird. His name was Wind Blower. When the bird flapped his mighty wings,

1

the wind roared down across the Dawnland, howling over the water, tossing the tree branches.

One day, Gluskape set out to hunt sea duck. However, the wind blew hard and rocked his canoe. White foam flew from the wave-tops, and the sea birds sat huddled against the rocks. The fish dove deep to escape the storm, and all Gluskape's arrows fell wide. "I'll try again tomorrow," he said, returning to Grandmother Woodchuck's warm fire.

The next day, the wind was raging and howling, and Gluskape could not hunt. Day after day, the tempest blew. Day after day, the hunters could not find food and they grew hungry. Gluskape said to his grandmother, Ngumee, "The Wind Blower has done this. I'll find him."

Feeling his full power, Gluskape rose up as high as the tallest pine tree. He strode northward to find Wind Blower. He walked for many days, even weeks, until he found the Wind Bird, a huge, white bird perched high on a rocky crag.

"Grandfather," Gluskape said respectfully, "You should show compassion for your grandchildren. The wind is too strong. We cannot hunt. Be easy with your wings."

However, Wind Blower scowled down at him with fierce golden eyes, his huge beak curved like an eagle. "I have been here since ancient times, long before you, long before anyone. My voice was the first. I was the first to create sound, the howling of my voice in the trees, the roar of my voice on the waters, the crying of my voice in the cliffs. I will beat my wings as I wish. Be off!"

Then Gluskape grew angry. In his power, he rose up in height as high as the clouds, and seized the bird as though he were a little sea duck. Gluskape bound his wings with a moose-hide thong, and threw him deep in a chasm between the rocks. He left him there.

It had taken Gluskape several weeks to find Wind Blower, but it took him only a few days to hurry home, as it is with all journeys. Now the people could go out in their canoes all day long. The water was flat and calm and the surface of the sea shone like blue glass beads. The ponds shone like flecks of mica, glinting in the warm sun.

Week after week, month after month, not a breeze tipped the leaves, nor tickled the ponds, nor whispered in the tall grasses by the sea. Flies droned in the still air. The lake waters became stagnant. Dead insects lay trapped in the brown scum that covered the ponds. Fish gasped at the surface, their gills beating for air. The water grew so thick that Gluskape could not paddle his canoe. Once more, the people grew hungry. That night, he said to Ngumee, "I must go back to find Wind Blower."

Day after day, he strode north again. His faithful loons had changed into their fog shape, and they loped beside him, one black, and one white. He found Wind Blower as he had left him, trapped in the rocks. Gluskape raised high as the clouds and lifted the giant bird. He sat Wind Blower back on the rocks and untied one of his wings. Then, with one sweep of his wing, Wind Blower sent a cooling north wind to the Dawnland. Gluskape's loons changed shape, and flew south as the breeze bent the trees and lifted the waves, and Gluskape hurried home to hunt sea duck, harmony restored.

He Who Was Unborn- The Giant Killer

(Micmac, Nova Scotia, recorded in 1871)

In olden times, there were giants in the woods, fierce and cruel giants. In the Micmac language, some were called Kukwesk. Their name means The Ones Who Were Always Hungry. The Kukwesk were huge and hairy, and they were greatly feared for they tracked and killed the People.

Once, a young Kukwesk saw a woman in the woods. He fell in love with her, even though she was a Micmac and not a giant. He wanted to marry her but he was very worried about what his father would say when he heard of this. Still, the young giant knew he would have to talk it over with his father.

"You can marry this woman of the People, but only on one condition- that I never, ever see her nor smell her," roared the grizzled old giant. "She must obey our laws. If she doesn't, then who knows what will happen?"

The young giant built a huge stone wigwam to hide his new wife in and told her she must stay there so that his father would never see her. Every day, the young Kukwesk set out to hunt, for he had to provide animal meat for his wife and her parents, but he also had to help in the tracking of the People.

Soon, the giant and his wife had a son. The young Kukwesk worried terribly that the food for his wife and son would become mixed up with his food. Therefore, he hung his food in a pouch made of bear gut far apart from their food.

"Never touch this," the young giant warned his wife and son every day as he left to go hunting. Every day, he reminded them.

Now, his wife was pregnant again. One afternoon, as she lay resting, the little boy began to play with his bow and arrows. He grew restless in the stone wigwam and leaped about, knocking things over, shooting wildly with his bow.

"Be careful!" cried his mother. "Never shoot your little arrows at the bear-gut pouch. That is your father's food. Stay away from it! You know better!"

Instead, defiantly, the little boy set his arrow, aimed and let it fly. The arrow pierced the sack of food and oil began to drip out.

"Ohh," moaned the boy's mother. "That is the end of us."

Quickly, she set a birchbark bowl beneath the sack to catch the oil, trying to set things right. Meanwhile, out in the forest, the young Kukwesk sank to the ground. With his power, he could see what was happening at home. In moments, his giant's strength was weakening. He knelt on the ground, resting his head on his bow, full of grief.

At last, he got to his feet and started home. Because he was so weak, it took him all day to walk back. He reached the stone wigwam and stumbled inside.

"Wife, you should not have let this happen," he said sadly, as he fell asleep. "You have broken your promise. Who knows what will happen now?"

In the morning, he went to the wigwam of his parents, his mother and father Kukwesk. He bent his head and entered. There they sat, ugly, old, greasy and hairy.

"We know what your son has done," roared his father angrily.

"Father," he said, "You may have my wife for food."

Then he went deep into the forest.

"Ahhh!" roared the old Kukwesk, full of rage and grief.

The power of the giants had come up on him. He leaped up. He strode to the old stone wigwam, entered it and killed the wife of his son, a woman of the People. He put her body on his toboggan and dragged it through the snow, stopping to throw her unborn child into the spring of water. There the unborn child floated, held up safely by the Turtle Person.

Back at the wigwam, the older boy cried and cried. When his father returned from the woods, he said, "Father, Grandfather Kukwesk came and killed my mother."

The young giant sat down, held the boy, and rocked him and rocked him until he finally went to sleep.

In the morning, his father said, "Go to the spring and bring us some fresh water."

The little boy took the birchbark bowl and hurried along the snowy path to the spring. Green moss circled the warm water, melting the snow. There, floating in the water, the little boy saw a tiny child laughing at him. It was his brother.

The older boy was overjoyed.

"Come out and play with me!" he cried happily. "It's all right! We're brothers!"

All day, they played by the spring. However, when they heard the crashing sound of their father coming home through the woods, the little one returned to the water and hid.

The older boy ran back to the stone wigwam and sat by the fire with his father. That night, he asked, "Father, can you make me two little bows and little arrows?"

So, the father sat by the fire, making the bows and arrows for his son. The next morning, the boy took them to the spring. The little one was waiting for him and leaped from the water. Together, they played in the woods, and then they ran to the stone wigwam. In there, they made a mess, jumping, leaping and throwing things around.

When they heard the giant's heavy footsteps returning home, the little one took the bows and smashed them to bits. Then he ran back to the spring and jumped in, helped again by the Turtle Person.

"What has happened here? Who has made this mess in the wigwam?" asked the giant. "Who has been here, playing with you?"

"It's my younger brother," said the boy. "He was thrown into the spring when

7

Mother died and he comes out to play with me. But, he won't stay. He is wild. Whenever he hears you coming, he jumps back into the water. I would like him to stay, though," the boy continued, "I think if we collect many feathers of all kinds, he will want to stay and play with them."

Therefore, the Kukwesk, still mourning the loss of his wife and hoping to make his only son happy, went into the forest to collect feathers from birds' tails. When his father had a big fistful of them stuffed into his pouch, the older boy once again lured his brother into the wigwam to play.

Three times, the little one came to play but escaped and ran back to the spring when he heard the giant coming. However, the fourth time, the older boy caught him and held him tight, while the little one kicked and struggled to break free.

The giant entered the wigwam and the little boy began to cry. Quietly, the Kukwesk sat down and held out a beautiful feather. The little boy snatched it and threw it in the fire, still crying. His father pulled out another from his pouch. Still, the little boy threw it in the fire. One after another, he threw each feather into the fire, crying and kicking, and trying to escape.

Finally, only one feather was left. The Kukwesk pulled it slowly from his pouch, hoping the little one would take it. It was a heron's feather, a tail feather, and He Who Was Unborn took it, laughing. He loved the heron feather.

Then the three of them lived together. The father brought the little one gifts from the woods each day for the boys to play with.

But He Who Was Unborn grew. He grew very fast and was full of power. One day, his father made him a bow, but when the Unborn One pulled it, it broke at once because he was so strong. So he had to make his own bow, and that bow was ten times stronger than any bow the People had.

He led his brother to the spring.

"Listen to me. I was not even born when our father let Grandfather Kukwesk kill our mother," he said.

"Yes," said the brother, "but she broke her promise. We touched the Kukwek's food sack."

"Nevertheless, it was wrong. Come with me. Her death must be avenged."

The brothers went into the woods and gathered load after load of birchbark. They carried all of the birchbark and placed it in and around the stone wigwam.

When their father, the giant Kukwesk, cannibal giant, returned that night, he was tired. He lay down by the fire and fell asleep.

Then He Who Was Unborn set fire to all of the birchbark and burned the stone wigwam. When the fire had cooled, he took two big stones, one from the spring and one from the doorway, and gathered up his father's bones, the power of the cannibal giant still in them. Then he ground the giant's bones to powder. The powder of the big bones, he tossed into the air, and the dust became flies. The powder from the smaller bones became mosquitoes and the powder from the tiniest bones became sand flies.

His father was dust blowing; nothing more.

"And now," said He Who Was Unborn, "We shall free the People from all the awful Kukwesk, the cannibal giants."

"Come," he said to his brother. "Let us go."

Gluskape, the Giant Killer, and the Whales

(Micmac, told in 1871)

All his life, Gluskape battled the giants, and so did his friend, He Who was Unborn. Slowly, they began to drive the giants from the land, moving them far to the north.

The two powerful friends loved to tease and test each other's power to see who was stronger.

He Who Was Unborn invited Gluskape to stay with him for a while on Partridge Island near St. John, New Brunswick. So, Gluskape and Grandmother Woodchuck came and were his guests.

At night, they sat by the flickering fire. The yellow flames danced like the little people dance in the summer sun. A thousand stars spread across the sky like a handful of tossed sand that was the spirit path of those who had died. The moon rose, shining on the pale blue clouds that swam across the night sky like a pod of whales.

Grandmother looked at the power in the cloud shapes and then spoke.

"I am remembering when young Marten and I were kidnapped by the magic witch, Winpe. She took us all the way to Newfoundland. I thought we would never get home. When Gluskape came after us, he sang a song to the whales, singing and singing, until a mighty female whale came. Gluskape knew she could swim fast. 'Take me across the water,' cried Gluskape, and the whale agreed.

He stood on her huge head, and quickly she swam across the Bay of Fundy and along Nova Scotia for hundreds of miles. However, this great whale was very much afraid of shallow water, for many whales die that way.

'Are we near land?' she called out.

'No,' answered Gluskape, the liar. 'Not yet.'

But the whale looked down and saw clamshells lying beneath her. She knew that she was near shore. As she swam above them, the clams began to sing a song, hoping to warn her and to trick Gluskape that way. They sang silly songs in squeaky voices and low voices. La, la, la. Lo, lo, lo. La, la, la. Lo, lo, lo.

Gluskape heard them.

'I understand their song. The clams, your friends, are telling you to hurry over the water,' he said to the whale. Once again he lied. His name meant 'liar.'

But she believed him. He was the great Gluskape, after all. So, the big whale swam like the wind. She swam right up onto shore and Gluskape stepped off onto dry land. Then the whale realized what had happened. She was in shallow water!

The whale cried out in sorrow, 'I shall die now. You tricked me.'

However, Gluskape laughed. 'Do not be afraid, Grandmother Whale. You will swim in the sea once more.'

He gave her a gift. He pulled out a pipe and some tobacco. He put the pipe in her mouth and pushed her back out to sea. Happily, the whale swam away, smoking the pipe as she went. Gluskape stood on the shore and watched her go, leaning on his bow. The smoke from the whale's pipe made a long, low cloud that followed her until she vanished in the far away.

"And that's my story," said Grandmother Woodchuck.

"I have seen trails of smoke follow whales," said He Who Was Unborn. "Thank you for the story. But now, I'm restless. Gluskape, let's go out to sea by torchlight and catch a whale."

"Alright," said Gluskape, for he was a brave and bold fisherman.

They lit a pine torch and walked down to the shore. The beach was full of great, gray boulders. He Who Was Unborn looked around and picked up the biggest one. For a joke, he set it on top of his head and turned it into a canoe.

Gluskape laughed loudly at the sight. Other giants heard the noise and came to the shore to watch.

"That's nothing," said his friend. "Watch this."

He Who Was Unborn took a piece of rock ripped from the granite ledge and turned it into a paddle. He took a second piece and made a spear. "Now," said He Who Was Unborn, "We're ready."

"Who will paddle in the stern and who will spear?" Gluskape asked.

"You paddle, and I'll spear."

So, they jumped into the stone canoe, and Gluskape paddled out to sea in the flickering torchlight. Soon their canoe passed on top of the biggest whale in the entire ocean.

He Who Was Unborn stood up, and he plunged the spear like a thunderbolt down into the water. When the handle rose up again above the surface, he seized it and caught the great whale as it thrashed and splashed. He Who Was Unborn grabbed the spear with both hands and twirled the great whale above his head. Finally, he plucked the whale from the spear and tossed him into the canoe as though he were a little trout.

All around the Dawnland, other giants had been watching. They laughed and laughed when He Who Was Unborn twirled the great whale. Then Gluskape paddled the canoe back to Partridge Island. He Who Was Unborn took a stone knife and split the whale in two with one blow. He gave half to his guests, Gluskape and his grandmother, and they roasted their side of the whale over the fire and ate it for supper.

The Chenoo's Icy Heart

(Micmac, Passamaquoddy, told by Louis Brooks)

In the olden times, before there were large tribes, a man and his wife went far off to the north one autumn to build their winter camp. They searched the woods carefully for a good spot to spend the winter, a spot with plenty of hardwood and a spring for water. There they built a dome-shaped winter wigwam out of birchbark.

The man brought home plenty of game – partridge, deer, and rabbit. The woman smoked and dried the meat, preparing for the long, cold months ahead. For some time, all went well for them.

One day, the man went out hunting. While his wife was gathering wood, she heard a rustling noise in the bushes. Startled, she looked up. She saw an awful face staring at her. It was part beast, part human, and haggard, gray and wolfish. His lips looked as if they had been chewed upon in a frenzy of hunger. The beast's body was covered with pine tar, and he had rolled on the ground until he was covered with sticks, pine needles, and leaves, which were all matted into his shaggy hair. He carried a bundle on his back.

The woman froze. She had heard of the terrible Chenoo, the ghoulish icy creatures that came from the far north. She saw at once that this was one of them. She knew she was in terrible danger, so she made a quick decision. Instead of showing fear, she walked slowly toward him, speaking warm words.

"Greetings, grandfather. How glad I am to see you."

The Chenoo reared up in surprise. He had expected yells, screams and stones. In wonder, he let the woman lead him into their wigwam. She was a wise woman, quick-witted and respectful. She brought him inside and seated him.

"Grandfather," she said, "I am so sorry to see you looking so tired and weary. You are dirty and look like you have traveled a long way."

She brought him some of her husband's clothes, and helped him dress himself and get clean. Then he sat by the side of the wigwam, surly and still. He did not move. This was all new to him.

The woman went out to gather more firewood. Abruptly, the huge Chenoo got to his feet and followed her. When she saw this, her heart pounded with fear and the blood roared in her ears.

"Now he will kill me," she thought, "My death is near."

The Chenoo walked slowly up to her. She turned and faced him bravely.

"Give me the axe," he said.

Calmly she handed him the axe, thinking all was over. However, to her surprise, he began to chop down trees. She had never seen such chopping! Pines fell right and left as though a storm had blown through the forest.

"Grandfather, that's enough!" she called out.

The Chenoo laid the axe on the ground and walked into the wigwam. He sat in the corner in grim silence. The woman kept on gathering sticks, just on the other side of the birchbark wall. Finally, as the sun sank low and red through the trees, she heard her husband coming. She ran through the woods to tell him what had happened.

"I think it best if we treat the Chenoo kindly," she said, and he agreed.

The husband parted the door flap and entered the wigwam.

"Father-in-law, how have you been?" he asked.

The Chenoo didn't answer. The man sat down beside him and began to talk. He told the Chenoo of all the things that had happened to their tribe over the years. As he listened to the stories, the Chenoo's fierce and angry eyebrows smoothed over, his cheeks relaxed and his mangled lips slowly closed over his grinning teeth.

Quietly, the woman took the husband's game bag and prepared a stew in the pot.

They offered the Chenoo a bowl of food, but he refused to eat. Instead, he lay down and went to sleep. The man and his wife lay down too, but they stayed awake in terror all night, watching the shadows leaping on the wall as the fire burned low. They were thinking that at any moment, the grisly Chenoo would jump up and kill them.

For three days, the Chenoo stayed in the wigwam, always away from the fire. He could not stand the heat. Day after day, he was sullen, grim and silent. He scarcely ate any of the food that the wife prepared.

On the fourth day, he seemed to change. He asked the woman for any fat she had. They had a large store of tallow saved for the winter. He filled the stew kettle with it and heated it on the fire. When it was scalding hot, he drank it in one hot, liquid gulp. Drinking hot fat was something the Eskimos do when they are sick and weak and when they have very little food.

At once, he turned ghostly pale. He turned his head to the wall and vomited up horrible creatures – ghouls, specters, serpents, and demons – that crawled away in the dirt like beetles and lice.

Finally, the Chenoo grew calm and slept for hours. After that, he ate food with the couple and was kind and good. The man and woman no longer feared for their lives and things went well.

All through the long winter, they ate dried and smoked meat. When spring came, the Chenoo foresaw that something terrible was going to happen. His enemy, a huge fierce female Chenoo, was coming with the last blast of the icy north wind. She was coming to kill him. He listened. From far, far, away, he heard her awful screams.

The family sat by the fire while he told them what would happen.

"The female Chenoo is far more terrible than the male. She will rip trees from their roots, and tear the ground itself apart. There is no end to the awful things she can do. It all depends on how large and icy her heart is."

The husband and wife looked at each other in fear.

"How can we help you?" asked the wife.

"You must hide in safety, and above all, you must never hear the terrible war whoop of the Chenoo. It is so horrible and loud a scream that, if you hear it, it alone can kill you. You must hide underground in a cave and stop up your ears." Then he said, "Daughter, go to the bundle I brought with me when I first came. It is hanging in a tree. If there is anything terrible in it, throw it away, but bring me the small bundle wrapped inside."

The wife hurried out of the wigwam and found the Chenoo's bag latched to a tree. She threw away the remains of the Chenoo's old meals – some human legs and feet – and carried the small bundle into the wigwam. The Chenoo unwrapped a soft piece of tanned deer-hide and brought out a pair of serpent's horns. One was branched like an antler and the other was straight and smooth. They were bright gold in color.

He handed the straight horn to the man. "Here. You will be my ally. This is a magic weapon full of power, from the head of a horned serpent that lives beneath the earth. It is the only weapon that can destroy a Chenoo."

So they prepared for the terrible ice creature. They dug a deep hole in the ground and waited for three days. As the Chenoo sat waiting, his face grew fierce and his old power came upon him once more.

Suddenly, he raised his head. From far, far away, he heard the awful scream, like no other sound on earth. It was the female Chenoo as she sped along the north wind. He heard her coming long before the people could.

He said, "If you can survive the first deadly scream, you will not be harmed. You must prepare for that. Should you hear me call for help, then hurry out with the horn, my friends, and you will save my life."

The man and wife stopped up their ears with melted fat and climbed into the hole they had dug. They squatted in the damp dirt, trembling and waiting, hidden under branches and leaves. A cold north wind roared through the trees above them. The trees nearly fell to the ground. They heard the terrible shriek of the female Chenoo, deafening and frightening, louder than screaming thunder.

The man and wife lay huddled in the hole, their hands clapped to their ears, which rang with pain. Despite the care they had taken, the scream nearly killed them. Their arms and legs turned cold and icy. Then, they heard the answering roar of their friend, and they knew they would live.

The battle of the Chenoo began.

The monsters, filled with their raging, icy power, rose to the size of mountains, stumbling among the clouds. They ripped pines from the ground to use as weapons. Earthquakes trembled in the ground and rockslides thundered in the hills. On and on it went, all day. The sky darkened as the male and female Chenoo battled. They stabbed each other repeatedly with pine trees. The female Chenoo ripped off the male's lip.

Finally, the husband and wife, still hiding in the hole, heard their friend call out "Son-in-law, come help me!"

Bravely, the man seized the magic horn and ran to the fight. It was a terrible sight. The Chenoos, as tall as clouds, lay wrestling on the ground, and the female was winning. She held the male Chenoo pinned to the ground while she tried to shove her magic horn in his ear.

To avoid death, the male thrashed his mangled face from one side to the other while she laughed at him.

"Stop your screaming! You have no son-in-law to help you. You are alone. And you will die!"

The Indian was so small compared to the giants that the female Chenoo didn't see him. She bent down low over the male, ready to take a bite from his shoulder.

The male Chenoo called out, "Now! Thrust the magic horn in her ear."

The man raised the horn over his head and struck hard. The point of the horn entered her head. At the touch, a flash of lighting darted straight through her, and she let out a blood-curling roar of pain. When the lightning touched the ground, it turned into a tall pole, pinning her head to the dirt.

"Touch the other end of the horn to a tree," the male cried.

When the man did this, the horn revealed its serpent power, and coiled rapidly around and around the tree like a snake. Now the female giant was caught fast. With the fury of the battle over, both Chenoos shrank to their normal size. Then they had to butcher the female Chenoo, for she needed to be destroyed to prevent a new Chenoo from springing forth from her bones.

The hardest job was melting her heart. It was made of a hard chunk of blue ice, much denser and colder than any ice known to man. It was so cold that fire could barely melt it. The woman brought birch-bark and pine branches and they built up a huge blaze. When they finally threw the icy heart into the fire, the flames sputtered, smoked, and hissed, and nearly went out. Slowly, the icy heart of the terrible Chenoo began to melt. Now they could chop at it with their hatchets and break it into bits. Finally, all the fragments had melted.

The next day, spring thaw came to the Dawnland. All over the forest, there was the sound of things melting and water dripping. Melted snow ran down the rivers to the sea and fell in soft lumps from the trees. Ice on the ponds split and cracked like muffled thunder.

It was time. The man and wife packed up their winter camp and headed for the seashore. The Chenoo went with them. They padded down the swollen streams, while he traveled through the woods far ahead of them. Each night the Chenoo made up camp for them and built their fire, then sat waiting for them to arrive.

For several days, the Chenoo did this. Moving south, a great change came over him, for the Chenoo was a creature of the far north, of howling winds and great darkness. He could not endure the gentle air of summer. The Chenoo grew smaller and weaker every day, until the husband and wife took turns carrying him like a little child. His terrible wounds had now healed, but his power had left him.

As they reached the shore where the tribe gathered, the People surrounded the giant in wonder and watched. As his eyes closed for the last time, the Chenoo shed a single tear. The gentle giant died.

Loon Woman

(Micmac, recorded in 1894)

In the times of the old ones, there was an encampment deep in the forest by the shore of a long, long lake. In addition, even farther up shore, even deeper in the woods, lived a poor family with two children, and older boy and a younger girl.

This boy and girl loved to go down to the lake and go fishing. Each one would catch a fish and call to each other.

"Can you tell what kind of fish I've caught?" the boy asked.

With her vision, she knew. "Of course I know," the girl replied. "It's a trout."

Then she caught a fish.

"Do you know what I've caught?" she called.

"A salmon?" asked her brother.

"No! It's a rainbow trout. I have beaten you, older brother," she said. Her power was a little stronger than his power.

Every day, the children played and fished along the shore. One day, they heard a sound.

"Hoo, hoo, hoo," they heard, far off in the distance. "Hoo, hoo, hoo."

It was Kwimu, Loon Person, calling and calling, a long lonely sound. The little girl listened to the hooting sound. It seemed to pierce right through her. She felt cold and lonely, as though she must linger by the lake. But she shook off the mood.

"Let's go home, brother," she said instead.

They picked up the trout they had caught and carried the fish back to their wigwam for their mother to cook. From that day on, the two children stayed closer together and from time to time heard the loon.

They built their own small wigwam to play in. In there, they sat and talked together. On and on, they talked. However, the others in the tribe could not understand it. They thought the children were foolish.

One day, the boy said to his sister, "I am going to make you some clothes. And then we will see what happens."

It was autumn and the maples stood red and orange. The birch leaves were yellow; the oak leaves golden brown. The boy made a colorful robe of leaves, red, yellow and orange. All kinds of leaves, all sizes and colors were in the robe. Then he wrapped her in it and led her to the shore of the lake.

"Now we are ready," he said. "I think something's going to happen. Walk up and down here. I will hide in the bushes."

So, she walked slowly up and down the lakeshore, wearing the robe of leaves. Suddenly, she heard a sound again.

"Hoo, hoo, hoo."

It was Kwimu, Loon Person, calling and calling; swimming closer and closer. He stared at the leaves of the cape.

Politely, the girl asked, "Grandfather, where have you come from?"

"From nowhere in particular."

The Loon had spoken directly to her! She ran off to find her brother. He came down to the shore with her and stood behind her to watch.

"What is it you wish?" asked Kwimu.

"We don't want anything," they said together, which was a respectful answer to his question.

Now, Kwimu swam even closer as he talked to them. He told these two poor children all about power. Afterward, the girl sat by herself in a rock at the edge of the lake. She sat thinking and thinking. Whenever she heard the call of the loon, she felt lonely. And, power grew in her through this lonely thinking.

Kwimu visited her almost every day. He was her spirit helper, her ally. He talked and talked with her.

One morning, as the mist drifted off the lake, the girl walked down to the rock. Kwimu, Loon Person, was already waiting for her.

"Death is coming," he said. "It is Kukwes, the cannibal giant."

She stared at him in fear.

"You must leave here. Tell your father and mother. Tell your brother. Take apart your wigwam. Kukwes, the Giant Who Is Always Hungry, will devour your whole camp. I have foreseen it. Take all of your things to the other side of the lake, and when you hear the terrible screams of the approaching Kukwes, go into the water and hide."

The girl ran home and told her family everything that Kwimu had said.

"We must go at once," said her father.

They listed the sheets of birchbark off the wigwam and packed their wooden kettle, bows, snowshoes, bone needles and skins. They bundled everything up. From down the shore, the other Micmacs watched. Their sagamore came out.

"Where are you going? Why are you leaving?" he asked as he approached their camp.

"Kukwes, the cannibal giant, is coming," said the children's father. "The whole camp will be destroyed."

"How do you know this?" asked the sagamore, frowning.

"Kwimu the Loon has told my daughter."

"Ha, ha, ha!" laughed the chief. "Loons, ha! Loons aren't important, and your daughter is nothing."

The poor family turned their backs on the sagamore and lifted their bundles. They hurried away from the big camp, circling the lakeshore, and started up the other side. They walked for hours until they heard the Kwimu call three times.

"Hoo, hoo, hoo."

Then they stopped and set up their wigwam close to the shore.

In the morning, Kwimu called to the children.

"Death is coming. In the evening, you will hear the awful scream of the Kukwes.

You must wade deep into the water, all of you, and hide there."

Sure enough, after the sun went down, the Bear Stars came out, and Old Man Star shone in the north, the family heard the terrible scream of the giant Kukwes. Then, they heard echoing across the water, awful shrieks of the People who had stayed behind. Men were shouting and women crying, and all the while, the awful Kukwes screamed and screamed.

The family waded deep into the dark lake, their heads tipped back, until only their eyes and noses showed above the cold, black water. All night long, they waited in the water scarcely breathing, trembling and hiding from the enemy. When the sun rose in the east above the bare treetops, they crept out of the water, shivering with the cold. They stood all alone on shore.

All around them was silence. No voices could be heard from the old camp. No smoke rose from the cook fires. No babies cried. No dogs barked. Slowly, the family crept to the edge of the camp. Everyone was lying dead. The awful Kukwes had destroyed them all.

The family hurried back to their new camp. Once more, Kwimu, Loon Person, talked to the boy and girl. He taught the boy to run as fast as the wind. He taught him to walk on water. He taught him to fly through the air.

With such a powerful hunter, the poor family now did very well. Still, Kwimu visited the girl, sometimes in his loon shape and sometimes as a man. He wanted to marry her.

"The lake is where you live. If you live with me, you will have everything you wish for," he said to her.

She looked at his shiny, black-feathered cape and the beautiful shell necklace around his throat. She remembered the loyalty and devotion he had given her and her brother. Still, she felt shy.

"I am not sure," she said.

That night, she spoke with her mother.

"He would be a good husband. He is kind and loons have great power. He helped you the whole time you were growing up," her mother answered. "Marry him."

Her brother gave her a stone knife, her mother gave her a piece of soft, tanned deerskin, and her father gave her a necklace of dyed porcupine quills. The girl left her family and walked deep into the lake with her new husband, Kwimu.

Now she had become Loon Woman. Sometimes she left the lake and visited her family on the shore. One day, she brought a speckled egg with her to show her family.

Her mother opened a medicine bag lined with soft feathers. They carefully set the egg in the bag and waited for the baby to be born. Everything was going so well for them.

One day, Kwimu said, "Danger is coming. I have seen it. Men are coming who will hunt me and kill me."

"Hide behind the large rock that sits in the middle of the lake," said Loon

Woman. "Hide there and I'll talk to them and see what they want."

In the morning, two men in a canoe visited the family.

"You must be lonely here," they said. "There are so few people hereabouts. Why not visit us across the lake?"

However, later, Kwimu said, "Don't go with them, Loon Woman. Stay here."

Therefore, her parents set off across the lake with her brother, but Loon Woman stayed behind because she was pregnant.

All this time, Kwimu had been teaching her brother power. Now, he did everything well- hunting, fishing, running, snaring birds and shooting. The strange men were jealous and decided to kill him.

During the night, Kwimu the Loon called to the young man, "Death is coming," warned the Loon. "Run away."

Quietly, the young man woke his sleeping parents and led them down to the lake. They climbed into the canoe and paddled away quietly that no one could hear the drips of water that fell from the paddle blade. They picked up Loon Woman and paddled up the lake, northward.

But, Kwimu said, "It is not far enough. Come farther up the lake or they will find you."

The brother and sister climbed back into the canoe, but their mother and father were tired and said that they would follow the next morning. While the parents were sleeping, the two men found them and killed them.

So, the brother, sister, and Kwimu lived at the far end of the lake. Loon Woman had a little daughter.

Kwimu told them, "I will stay with you for seven years. Then I must return to the land of Kwimu. But, I will always guard over you."

When the seven years were up, he said goodbye and disappeared into the loon world.

Every day, his loyal wife walked the shore, mourning him. She felt her heart breaking with loneliness and devotion. In the distance, she heard the wild cry of a loon echoing off the surrounding hills, and she felt sadder still.

Then one day, she saw Loon Person, swimming under water. The loon broke the surface and leaped ashore as a man running toward her. It was Kwimu, her husband!

"I couldn't stay away from you. I could not stop thinking of you. So, I have left the world of the loons to come back to you."

She was so overjoyed to see him. Together, they walked by the shore of the lake.

"If we stay together," said Kwimu, "This lake will give you all that you wish."

Gluskape and the Mighty Wasis

(Marie Sakis, Penobscot, Old Town)

In olden times, the people and animals of the Dawnland were one. They spoke the same language and understood each other. They lived in harmony.

When Gluskape stepped from his stone canoe onto the shore of the Dawnland, he called all the animals to him. He gave them each a name: he called the Bear "Mooin," the Squirrel "Miko," and Turtle was "Mikchik." The animal he didn't trust was Beaver, who could create great floods with his dams.

The animals were not the size they are now. They were very big. The beaver was more than six feet long. The squirrel was larger than the bear. Gluskape asked Mooin the Bear, "What would you do if you met a man in the woods?"

Mooin answered, "I fear him. I would run away."

And that was as it should be. So, Gluskape didn't change Bear's size. Instead, Gluskape picked up Miko, as big as he was, and patted him and smoothed him down until he grew smaller and smaller, until the squirrel was the size we see today.

Then Gluskape asked him, "What would you do if you met a man in the woods?"

Miko answered, "I would run up a tree and hide."

31

It was Moose's turn to be asked the same question, and Moose said, "I would run through the woods. I would hide." Beaver answered the same.

But, Gluskape never trusted Beaver. In those days, Beaver was a monstrous creature. The bones of these Beavers may be found today. Their teeth are six inches across and their bodies nearly ten feet long. These giant beavers built huge dams that filled the valleys.

After he had shaped the animals, Gluskape made the greatest creature, Man. He had to teach men to survive. He taught them to build huts and canoes, how to fish and build fires. He taught them how to live together, and told them not to gossip or be jealous and that power came with wisdom and respect. However, the people didn't always listen.

Even Gluskape himself could act foolish with pride, as you will soon see. Slowly, Gluskape was ridding the Dawnland of the terrible monsters, horned serpents, sorcerers and ice giants. He was teaching the people to grow crops, build weirs, cure meat, and make drums. The people were doing well. Gluskape felt proud.

He bragged to a Penobscot woman, "I am doing well. The Chenoo are nearly gone. The Kukwes too. Everyone has meat. My people prosper."

The woman looked at him. "Not so fast," she said. "You think you have gotten rid of all the powerful creatures in the deep woods? Maybe. However, there is one creature you have not conquered. The Mighty Wasis will remain unconquered until the end of time."

"Ha! What a joke," laughed Gluskape. "Who might this be?"

She led him to her wigwam. Calmly, she pointed. "There sits the Mighty Wasis."

The beast was a baby. He sat on the floor of the wigwam sucking on a sweet piece of maple sugar, greatly content and in a world of his own. Gluskape, the hero and master of the Dawnland, had never married and had never raised a child. Since he had never raised a child, he was quite certain that he knew all about it, as people without children always think they are experts at such things. The woman knew this.

So, Gluskape knelt down and smiled a big smile at the Wasis. "Come here, little one," he said.

The baby smiled at him a little, but didn't move. So, Gluskape tried harder. He made his voice as sweet as the songs of summer birds. But, the Wasis ignored him and chewed on the maple sugar. This made Gluskape angry. He wasn't used to being ignored. Wasn't he lord and master of Dawnland?

"Come over to me at once," he bellowed.

The Wasis burst into tears, crying and yelling but still he did not move. That left Gluskape with only one choice, magic. So he used some powerful spells and even sang a song that can bring the dead back to life. The Wasis stopped crying and listened to the singing with curiosity and admiration. But he still did not move.

Gluskape threw up his hands. "I give up. I have been defeated."

Just then, a ray of light shone through the doorway of the wigwam. The Wasis looked at the patch of yellow sunlight.

"Coo, coo," the Wasis cried, waving his arms.

So if you see a baby call out, "Coo, coo" and you're not sure why, know that it is remembering the time when the Mighty Wasis overcame Gluskape, who had shaped and formed the world. For of all things since the beginning of time, the baby has been the only invincible one.

The Magic Giants

(Micmac, told by Nancy Jeddore, Nova Scotia, 1870)

In olden times, a man and woman lived by the sea, far from other people. They had many children and were very poor. Both parents traveled out in their canoe almost every day, hoping to catch birds and fish, and search the cliffs for eggs to feed their hungry children, who stood waiting for them on the rocky shore.

One day, while the parents were out in their canoe, a cold, dense fog blew in from the east. Within minutes, the parents were lost. They didn't know which way to paddle home. There was nothing to do but sit in the damp, cold fog, and wait, drift, and worry.

"The children are all alone," said the wife. "Will the older ones find berries and clams for the younger ones?"

The husband shrugged. "Perhaps the fog will clear soon and we'll be home before dark."

They sat staring into the fog. Sometimes their eyes played tricks on them. It seemed that they saw a shape, but moments later, the shadow vanished into the water droplets. The woman rubbed her eyes, which ached from the strain of staring into the fog. She thought of Killer Whale Person.

"Do you think," She asked, "That Killer Whale Person, the shape changer? and deceiver will find us here?"

The husband had his bow, but only a few arrows. The arrows would be useless against the mighty Killer Whale. Only last autumn, killer Whale Person had chased his brother-in-law's canoe and bit off the back end with one huge chomp.

"No," said the husband. He didn't want her to be afraid. "We are safe. I am sure of that."

So, they sat for hours floating on the sea, the Bay of Fundy with its twisting rocky shores and dense cold fogs. Suddenly, the wife cried out and pointed, "Look! Is it Killer Whale?"

The man saw a big, dark shadow approaching them, growing larger and larger. It was a canoe, but it was a big canoe full of giants. The couple stared with wide eyes, watching the eight giants paddle the big canoe toward them. The giant in front spoke to them courteously.

"Little brother, hello. Where are you going in this fog?"

Because the giant had spoken kindly, the man and wife knew that they were safe. So the man replied, "We are lost in this thick fog. We can't get home, and our children are alone without us."

"Don't worry," said the giant, "We'll take you in our canoe to our camp. My father is the chief. You will be well-treated."

The giants slid the blades of their paddles gently under the little canoe and lifted it aboard their big one. The husband and wife were amazed at their gentleness. The giants were pleased too, as though they had found two wonderful playthings, two dolls.

The giants paddled fast and soon the fog disappeared. Up ahead, the people saw three wigwams as high as mountains. The biggest giant of them all, the chief, came down to the shore to greet them.

"What have you found, my sons? Where did you find that little brother and sister?"

"Lost in the fog, far out to sea."

"Bring them into my wigwam," said the chief.

So one son picked up the canoe and set it in the palm of his hand with the man and woman still sitting inside it. He carried them into the chief's wigwam, and set them on a shelf way in the back. The chief was very kind. He bent over to talk with them in a soft voice.

"My name is Skun," he whispered. No doubt, his roar could be heard all over the Dawnland. "That means liver-colored. Liver is a gift, the place that gives power and life. Stay and share our food with us."

The giants went out hunting. The people were amazed when the giants came back with twenty caribou hanging from their belts, just as a Micmac might carry a string of small squirrels. One or two moose swung from their belts like little rabbits. The giants prepared a meal for their little friends, but they were careful not to feed them so much that they might burst.

Afterward, they sat in a circle about the fire. The giant chief, Skun, had power. He could foresee danger. Sagamores everywhere must know at once everything that is going on today, and what will be happening tomorrow.

"Once we were attacked by the Chenoo. His awful scream can kill people as small as you. His scream is full of the power of the icy north and it can freeze the blood in your veins if you are not prepared."

Skun was shaping a bow from the trunk of a tree as he told this. He scraped it with a large beaver's tooth. The tooth was ten times bigger than any tooth the people had seen.

"Once there were large animals roaming the forest- huge beavers and big bears with thick fur. The water was locked in ice and the ice giants were many. Gluskape has changed that. Still life is not easy. I see Death coming."

"What do you see father? Tell us," urged his sons.

"I see Kukwes, the cannibal giant; the One Who is Always Hungry. He will be here in three nights."

So the giants prepared for battle. Skun told the people to pour melted fat in their ears, and wrap themselves thickly in skins. The man and wife waited, rolled up in skins like two dolls, high on a dark shelf at the back of the wigwam.

On the third day, the roar of the cannibal giant, Kukwes, shook the giant's wigwam. The fire blew out from the sound. The stones around the fire shattered to bits. Huddled in the robes, the two Micmacs trembled as the roar filled their throats and stomachs. It seemed like the scream would kill them, and they knew the Kukwes had attacked the giants with all his power and fury. Suddenly the noises stopped. One last scream, they barely heard at all. Skun came to get them. It was over.

The giants returned from battle, all covered with blood. Their legs were pierced with huge pine trees and even oaks. Their arms were too. The giants sat by the fire and pulled out the trees as a person might pull out a splinter or nettles. They told how they had crushed the Kukwes's eye with a boulder and crushed his brain.

"It was a fearful battle," they said. After that, they rested and ate.

The next day, Skun asked the people if they were tired of their visit with the giants. "You have been very kind," said the man. "But our children are waiting at home for us, and we are worried about them."

"Tomorrow you shall go," said Skun.

The next morning their canoe was lifted down from the shelf and carried to the shore. The giants packed it full of moose, beaver, and otter meat, as well as thick furs. Then the chief brought out a little dog. The dog jumped in the canoe with them.

"This dog has the power to smell land and will point his nose in the direction you should go. You cannot get lost if he is with you."

The people thanked the giants for their kindness.

"You will remember me in seven years," Skun said and pushed them out to sea. "One day I will need your help."

So they set out, the woman on the bow, the dog in the middle, and the man at the stern. The sea was smooth and calm, and in no time at all, they saw their old wigwam. On shore, the children danced with joy, waving and pointing out the canoe to each other. The dog was happy too. He leaped from the canoe, barked, and played with the children as though he had always known them.

The parents hugged the children to them. They all agreed they wanted to keep the dog, but suddenly the canine turned and went back to Skun, his master, scampering across the sea as if it were as hard as ice.

After that, the poor family with the many children did much better. The father had gained great power from the giant Skun, his friend. He was a good hunter now. There was plenty to eat- fish, duck, and even moose.

Six years had passed, and the man and his wife had nearly forgotten how they had once been lost in the fog. In the seventh year, the man began to have many dreams. In some of the dreams, the man was in the Land of the Giants again. He dreamed also of a great whale, singing a sweet song to him. The man knew that the whale in his dreams was bringing him great power.

"I am changing," he said to his wife. "The power in my dreams is changing me."

"Will you become a spirit? Will you change from being a man?" she asked.

"No, I don't think so. I think the power of Skun has entered me."

The next day, the man knew that something was going to happen, but he didn't know what. He felt very restless and uneasy. The man and his wife sat outside their wigwam, looking out to sea. From the southwest, a shapechanger was coming. It was in the shape of Killer Whale with its black fin cutting through the water.

Killer Whale swam in close and stared at them, but he did not sing the sweet song of whales. His teeth were jagged and white, his jaw huge and fierce. Suddenly, he turned and swam off.

The man restlessly paced the shore. "Something has happened," he said. "I know it."

A few days later, Skun's little dog came running to them over the water. Happily, the children rushed outside to play with him, but the dog looked steadily at the man, waiting for a message. His tail was wagging.

"In three years, I will visit Skun," said the man.

The dog licked him and ran back over the water the way he had come. Three years later, the man got into his canoe and paddled fearlessly to the Land of the Giants. He saw the three huge wigwams standing on the shore and the big canoes were beached, drawn up on the shore. The giants were gone and the camp was silent. Then the man saw the old giant chief, Skun. He came down to greet the man.

"Yes, my friend. All my songs are dead. We were attacked three years ago by Killer Whale, the Deceiver."

Skun led the man into the wigwam and they ate a little together.

"It's good you have come, little brother. Once you needed me for help, but now I need you. I am alone now, and I am old. Soon I will die, but first, I want to leave something with you."

Skun got up and came back with and armload of his son's clothes.

"Put these on," said Skun. "Take them with you, and the power which filled my sons will fill you."

So the man donned the clothes. When he walked into the robe, it was like entering a dark cave. Once inside, great power filled him and he rose in size. Wisdom filled him. The man thanked Skun and took the clothing home in his canoe. He brought them back to his family. There he stayed, by the sea, with his wife and children.

Whenever he needed, he put on the clothes, and was filled with strength and knowledge.

Part 2

How Gluskape Found Summer

(Passamaquoddy, sung by tribesman, Noel Neptune)

A long, long time ago, when the People first lived in the early dawn-red land, before Squid's Neck was crowded with people the way it is now, Gluskape went far to the north where the land was still locked deep in glaciers of ice.

He came to a big wigwam where he found the great ice giant, Winter. Gluskape greeted Winter, entered the wigwam and sat down. Then Winter gave him a pipe and Gluskape smoked, while the giant told of ancient times. He wouldn't stop talking. A magic spell charm was put on Gluskape. It was a Frost spell. The ice giant talked on and on until Gluskape froze and went to sleep. He slept for six months like a toad.

When the spell broke, he awoke. Gluskape hurried home to the south. At every step, the air grew warmer and warmer, and flowers began to come out of the ground. The flowers talked to him and asked where he had been. He told them of the ice giant in the igloo far to the north.

Gluskape then came to a place where there were many Mikumwess, the magical little people, dancing in the forest. One of their daughters was named Summer. Summer was the most beautiful one ever born.

Gluskape watched her dancing in the warm yellow sunlight. Then he caught her, with a crafty trick and put her into a bag. He cut a piece of moose-hide sinew into a long cord and as he ran away with Summer, he let the end of the cord trail behind him.

The little people of the forest sunlight, the Mikumwess, pulled and tugged at the cord, but as Gluskape kept running the cord ran out, and he left the little people far behind.

Soon, he had returned to Winter's lodge. This time he had Summer carefully hidden in his shirt. This time he was prepared and felt powerful, ready to challenge Winter.

Winter welcomed him back in, hoping to freeze him back to sleep again, but this time Gluskape did the talking. This time, his m'teouin was stronger. Before long, the sweat ran down Winter's face, and he began to melt more and more and so did his wigwam. Gluskape had brought Summer to the far north!

Then everything awoke! Even the tundra bloomed with tiny flowers. The caribou swam in the lakes. The grass grew, the little people came out, and in the forests, the melted snow ran tumbling down the rivers washing away the dead leaves from last year.

Gluskape carried Summer far to the south. He left Summer with her own people as before, and returned home to Grandmother Woodchuck and his little brother, Marten.

The Thunders and Mosquito Person

(Micmac, Lucy Pictou, 1923)

In olden times, the Thunders were creatures who lived like men, but could change their size and shape should there be a storm. When their chief ordered them to put on their wings, they grew as large as Wind Blower, the giant sky bird. Then they would fly south, whipping up storm clouds, and throwing thunder bullets and hailstones. Some say the Thunders live up the east branch of the Penobscot River, high in a cave on Mount Katahdin, the great mountain. Others say their home is somewhere else in the sky.

After a big storm day, the Thunders were resting on a cloud before starting their long trip home. They were talking to Mosquito Person, sitting on that cloud.

"How is it that life is so easy for you? Where do you find such fine, fresh blood to drink?"

Mosquito Person thought to himself, "If I tell them it is the blood of the People, they will take it all, and I will have nothing."

Aloud, he said, "You see that big forest down below? I get my blood from the trees."

The Thunders jumped to their feet and whipped up a big storm cloud, white on top and purple-black on bottom. They threw a thunderbolt at the tree and split it from top to bottom, but there was no blood anywhere to be found.

The Thunders searched for Mosquito Person.

"You lied to us. There is no blood in trees."

"Something so wonderful is not so easy to find," replied Mosquito Person. "Try that tasty little tree over there."

Again, the Thunders clapped their wings. They struck the little tree and even killed a porcupine underneath it. They tasted the porcupine's blood but spat it out.

"Pfftew! That Mosquito Person is not telling us the truth. He's hiding something from us!"

They found Mosquito Person hiding in a swamp.

"Again, you have lied to us," they roared.

Mosquito Person looked a little worried. The Thunders were big. They glared at him with big gray eyebrows like heavy boulders. Their eyes were yellow like an eagle's.

Mosquito Person hummed his whiny little song. "The brook that runs to this swamp. Try that."

So the Thunders called up a big storm cloud and lightning struck the brook. Some fish died, lying on their sides in the shallow water. They tasted the fish blood.

" No, this is not it, either!" they roared at the annoying little insect.

"Sorry, sorry! Try the ocean. That's what I meant. There is much tastier blood in the ocean fish."

The Thunders flew off to the sea. Mosquito Person felt relieved. He thought he had been very clever this time and that it might take them quite a while to taste all the fish in the sea.

Meanwhile, the Thunders threw a lightning bolt at the sea and killed a shark. They spat out his blood. It tasted bitter and nasty, the worst blood of all.

Mosquito hovered nearby. "No, no," he buzzed. "Wrong kind of fish."

"Wrong kind of answer!" bellowed the Thunders, their patience at an end.

They grabbed Mosquito Person and turned him into a hailstone, but thanks to Mosquito Person's lies, the Thunders even today rarely strike the People of the Dawnland.

Mahtigwess the Rabbit Becomes Wise

(Micmac and Passamaquoddy, Tomah Josephs)

In olden times, Mahtigwess the Rabbit lived with his grandmother in the woods. It was mid-winter, and it had been a hard time for both of them. In their birch-bark wigwam, Rabbit and Grandmother sat around their small fire.

Hunger gnawed at Rabbit's stomach. Grandmother's fur robe was worn and thin. Ice lay thick on the lake and the crusted snow covered the ground. It was hard to find food.

"You must try harder to bring us food tomorrow," Grandmother said to Rabbit. "We are nearly starving."

I've tried hunting. I set snares. I'm tired of it. I think I'll ask someone for help," he said. "I'll do what they do and see how they get by. I'll visit Otter and see how it is that he stays so fat."

Grandmother shook her head, but said nothing in order to keep peace in the wigwam.

So the next day, running through the forest on his snowshoes, Rabbit came to Keeony the Otter's lodge. Otter's home stood on the edge of a lake on a steep bank. He had a built an ice-slide straight down into the water.

Otter came out and made Rabbit welcome. His fur was smooth and sleek, his stomach round and full.

"You're just in time for dinner, Rabbit. Come in," said Otter. "Sit down and wait. I'll be right back."

Then Otter took his eel-spear and went outside. He slid gracefully down the ice-slide and dove under the ice. Moments later, he was back with a spearful of plump wriggling eels.

Otter put them in his stew pot with some dried lily roots and berries and prepared a fine stew.

"This is a fine life you have," said Rabbit. To himself he wondered, "Why can't I do this if Otter can? I am much cleverer than he is."

"Otter," said Rabbit. "You must come to my house for dinner the day after tomorrow."

Rabbit hurried home and told his grandmother about what he had seen. She listened to the story of the ice-slide and the spear, but shook her head and said nothing.

The next morning, Rabbit rushed out and prepared to move their wigwam next to the lake. He packed all their belongings in no time, for once he started something he never gave up. In just one day, he had moved the wigwam and built an ice slide just like Otter's.

When Otter arrived for dinner, Rabbit grabbed a stick and leaped for the door. "Get the pot ready, Grandmother," he called. "I'll be right back."

However, at the top of the slide he stumbled. He tripped, slipped and fell. Down the ice slide he went, flipping and flopping, head over heels right into the lake!

Rabbit was a terrible swimmer, the worst of all animals really. He didn't have the right fur nor a sleek body lined with far like Otter's. The water was cold, and he very nearly drowned.

At the top of the slide, Otter watched in amazement. "What is he doing?" he asked.

"Oh, something he saw someone else do," said Grandmother Rabbit.

Quickly Otter slid into the water and pulled out Rabbit, who limped into the wigwam to get warm. Grandmother dried him off and gave him pine-needle tea. Otter took the stick and dove for eels, but he was angry at Rabbit for imitating him and threw the fish down at the door of Rabbit's wigwam. Otter went home without eating anything.

However, Rabbit had one virtue. He never grew discouraged and he never gave up. He was sure he could find an easy way to find food in winter. So he sat and thought for several days until all the eel stew was gone. He decided to visit Bear, the most magical and powerful of all animals.

"I will find out how Bear survives the winter without eating at all," he said to Grandmother. "He never even leaves his cave!"

She shook her head and sighed, but said nothing. So Rabbit went to visit Mooin the Bear in his cave.

"I'm delighted to see you, my friend," said Bear, glad of a visit or during the month of crusted snow. "You must stay for dinner."

"Thank you," said Rabbit. "I'd like nothing better."

So Rabbit sat down and Bear put a large kettle on the fire to boil. Then he cut a tiny slice from the bottom of his big thick footpad, for Bear is full of magic. He threw this piece in the stew pot and soon a flavorful stew was bubbling away, filling the cave with a delicious smell.

"This is a wonderful thing," thought Rabbit. They ate the stew and Rabbit said, "Now, Bear, come visit me for dinner the day after tomorrow."

When Bear arrived for dinner, Rabbit called out, "Put the pot on to boil, Grandmother. Soon we'll have a nice stew."

Then Rabbit sat down with his knife and tried to cut a slice from his thin, small footpad as Bear had done.

"Whatever is he trying to do?" asked Bear, frowning. Look how badly his foot is bleeding."

"Oh, something that he saw someone else do."

50

By now, Rabbit had cut his foot badly, for he was very persistent and determined to succeed. There was no dinner to eat either.

"This is nonsense. Give me the knife," growled Bear. With his magic, he prepared a tasty stew.

Afterward, Grandmother Rabbit soaked Rabbit's foot and wrapped it in a spruce gum poultice. But his paw was slow to heal. He could not rush about the woods on his snowshoes. He had to sit still and rest. Several weeks passed.

One night, Rabbit hopped to the opening of the wigwam and threw back the door-flap. He saw the thin trail of smoke from their fire that wandered up to the stars. He saw the Milky Way scattered like blue and white wampum beads across the sky, the ghosts of those who have died lived there.

He thought, "I cannot be an otter or a bear. Perhaps it was not Bear's paw that made the stew. Perhaps it was his m'teouin."

Rabbit went back inside and said to no one in particular, "With perseverance, anything is possible. It is even possible that a foolish Rabbit may become a wise one."

His grandmother burst out laughing. "Maybe," she said.

"So," said Rabbit. "I must go learn my own kind of power."

The next day, Rabbit set out. He went deep into the woods to learn all about nature. He studied the ways of animals and of man. He studied himself and learned how he had failed when he imitated others. He saw how different rabbits are from otters and bears. Because he never gave up, but tried and tried, slowly he became more powerful. Until at last, he became a powerful conjurer.

Then he returned home. Two years had gone by!

Grandmother Rabbit sat by the fire in her thin robe, nibbling dried berries and roots. She had had no meat to last her through the winter.

"Grandmother!" called Rabbit as he leaped high over the wigwam. "I'm back! Don't worry. I am here to take care of you. Sit down and eat. I'll make you a tasty stew." With a handful of pinecones and a kettle of water, he did just that.

Man Singing for Animals

(Micmac, Nova Scotia, 1923 told by Isabelle Googoo Morris)

Long ago, in olden times, there was a big camp of people by a river. They stayed there all the time. At night, they went torch fishing in the river and the whole river was bright with the light of their torches bobbing up and down. They speared salmon, trout, and eels.

In the forests nearby, they hunted moose. They dried and smoked the meat until it was nice and brown. They had a good life and saw no reason to change their ways. Every year they did the same things as the years before. This made the elders happy.

Two young men in the village had power. They felt restless as most young men do, and felt called to take a journey. They were not sure why. Perhaps it was to look for other people, to learn from them. So they prepared to leave the camp. They prepared their bows and made many arrows.

"When are you coming back?" the others asked.

"When we have found some other people to talk to. We will travel south and see what we find. We have power and will be safe."

So the young men walked for seven days, and then for seven more. Due to their power, they were safe from harm. One night, one of the young men began to smoke his pipe by the fire. He was listening for signs, listening for sounds, and his power filled him as he smoked.

"People are nearby," he said, blowing sacred smoke all around his head. "Come on."

They hadn't gone far when they saw a wigwam. They called out greetings and a voice answered, asking them to enter.

Inside they found a man and a woman. They sat together and smoked for a while.

"Where have you come from?" asked the man after a while.

"There is a large camp where we live by the river. Here, is there only you?"

"I have lived here since words began," said the man. "And this is my grandmother. She has been here since the world was made. We will eat first. Then, when the sun goes below the earth, I'll show you something."

The old woman prepared moose meat and ground nuts for them. Quickly she gathered up their spoons and bowls and put them all away again.

"Now, grandsons," she said. "Lie down against the wall. We need space to work. You may see something," and she put out the fire.

The sun sank below the earth and the man began to beat on a log and to sing. He had a birch-bark drum. He beat on the drum and sang, "I am the Man Singing for Animals. I am singing for the animals, to come alive, to come back to life. From all those parts of them, those wings, heads, feet. From those bones, meat and marrow. For all those parts of them that were not eaten, for all those parts that were thrown away."

He sang and sang and beat the drum. All night long, as the stars rose and passed across the sky and sank one more beneath the earth, he sang. When the sun rose, he stopped.

"This is my work every night," he said to the young men. "People cannot waste anything. Every part of the animals should be used. Every part of the animals must be respected. Even eel skins, even hair. What People cannot save or cannot use, they should bury with respect. We owe the animals everything. They give their lives to us."

54

The young men understood what they had seen. The man got up and stretched after his long night of drumming and singing. "Come on. I'll show you something more."

They went outside down to the shore where he kept his canoe. "Do you want to see the fish come?" he said. "Watch this."

From his pouch, he took out a whistle made of shell. He played music on it. The sea bottom was very clear, and the young men could see all kinds of fish coming to hear the music.

"These fish I made from all the parts of fish that the People throw away. I sing for them and they come back."

"Thank you," said the young men. "We can go home now. We have found what we were looking for."

Even now, every night the man is singing, the bones of the animals are brought back to life. He sings in the dark with no fire and no light. He takes out a moose bone and sings. The moose jumps out of the bone and runs away. He takes out a caribou bone and beats his drum. The caribou leaps up and runs away. He has bones of mink and beaver and bear. All of these come to life when he sings. The Man Who Sings for Animals makes them all alive again.

Partridge's Canoe

(Passamaquoddy, told by Tomah Josephs)

When a partridge, Plawej, beats upon a hollow log, he makes a noise like a man at work building a canoe. A man building a canoe, from afar, sounds like the drumming of a partridge's wings. All this is true because in olden times, the Partridge was a canoe builder for all the Bird People.

One day, all the birds assembled. Each one got into his boat and it was quite a sight to see. First, Eagle entered his great boat and paddled off using the tips of his wings as oars. Then came Owl, and he did the same. Then Crane, Bluebird, and Blackbird. Even the tiny Hummingbird had a little boat. For him, Partridge had made a pretty paddle, about one-inch long.

Fish Hawk circled above the sky. He cried out when he saw the parade of bird boats coming, paddling out to sea. Then Fish Hawk asked Partridge why he had not built a canoe for himself. He merely looked mysterious and drummed. So, the bird asked again, why he had no boat.

Finally, Partridge said, "When I build my boat it will be a wonder to see." He refused to say anymore. This silence went on for nearly a month. Partridge would not disclose his secret plan to anyone. Finally, Partridge announced that he was ready to

56

launch his boat.

All of the Bird People arrived on the banks of the river, eager to see what surprise Partridge had in store.

Off in the woods, in secret, Partridge had decided that if a boat that had two ends like a canoe could be rowed in two directions, then a boat that was round could be rowed in every direction. That would surprise everyone and they would all be jealous of his cleverness. So, he had built himself a boat that was perfectly round like a bird's nest.

He had hidden it under some bushes and now he pulled it out to show everyone. This canoe astonished the bird people, who had never thought of such a thing before. And he was pleased as everyone admired it.

Partridge climbed into his canoe and pushed off. He started to paddle, but to the astonishment of the birds, he made no headway at all. The boat simply turned round and around, again and again, no matter how he tried to move it forward. The birds began to laugh at the sight and Partridge felt ashamed. His boat went nowhere at all!

He left the riverbank and flew far inland. There he hid under low bushes and never sought the sea or rivers. Ever since he built his canoe, he had become an inland bird, and still is to this day.

How the Micmacs Found Plants

(Micmac)

In olden times, seven Micmac people were traveling across the mountains. They climbed down a sheer cliff face on one mountain and came to a meadow. In the valley was a long, narrow lake with a tiny island in the center.

The island was a canoe for them. They used a long pole to push their way across the lake. When they landed on the opposite shore, they saw Skunk Woman's wigwam. Skunk Woman came out to meet the travelers. She cooked for them and fed them a fine stew.

Skunk Woman had power. She took her grease bag made of skin and began to do a little swaying dance. She sang about a storm. "As far as I can see, I see a red sky. Red clouds, dangerous clouds, are coming." She was using her power to warn the Micmac men.

The men decided to leave Skunk Woman and return to the shore. "Before we go home, we want to spy on the other tribe and see how they live. Maybe we can find out their secrets."

The camp of wild people lived there all alone. No one had ever visited them before. The wild people were very fierce and killed anyone who tried to approach.

"They will kill you if they find you, "warned Skunk Woman. Then she gave the seven Micmacs the gift of her bag of grease.

58

As the men got back into their canoe, they saw something swimming toward them. It was Kikwesu, Muskrat Person. He was the watch-guard for the wild people. When he spotted these seven men, he cried out, "Warning! Look, Wild Ones! Strangers have come!"

"Sshh, quiet!" One man, Jay Person, cut a piece of fat from Skunk Woman's grease bag and tossed it to Muskrat Person, because muskrats love anything fatty. Muskrat stopped shouting and greedily gobbled it up.

"Now," said Jay Person, holding the bag up high. "Do you want more? Then go and steal for us one of the Wild People's canoes and bring it to us. We'll give you all the fat in the Skunk Woman's bag."

So, Muskrat swam across the lake and stole one canoe, which he brought to that man, Jay Person.

Jay Person thanked Muskrat. "I will cross now. It's very dark and the Wild Ones won't see me. I can watch them dancing. The rest of you wait here. Maybe I can find out their secret."

Muskrat gobbled up the grease and licked his paws. He said, "I'll go too. I can bite holes into all of their canoes and paddles. Then I'll get an old tree stump and drag it through the water. In the darkness, they will think it is a moose swimming, and they will chase it in their canoes. So let me go first."

The Micmac agreed that this was a good plan to trick the Wild People. Muskrat swam off to bite holes in all the canoes and paddles. Jay Person paddled across the lake and went ashore. He heard the sounds of dancing coming from inside a large wigwam. He tiptoed up to a hole in the side and peeked through. He stuck his beak, right into that hole to watch the pretty girls dancing inside.

An old woman sat in there as well. She said, "What is that thing sticking through the hole? It looks like a beak. I'll burn it with a stick and see if it moves! Ha, ha!"

She took a stick from the fire and touched it to Jay's nose. It burned terribly.

"Yee-ow!" Jay Person fled back to the island where his friends were waiting. They all laughed at him as he slapped cool mud on his sore nose. But they were angry too because he had learned nothing of the secrets guarded by the Wild Ones.

"Never mind," said Muskrat. "Their canoes are full of holes. Let me go back and pretend to be a moose."

The moon rose. Moonlight shone on the lake and Muskrat swam out, pulling an old tree stump through the water. One old Wild Person saw him swimming in the moonlight path and saw the twisted roots of the stump crossing the lake.

"A moose! A moose is swimming across the lake. Come on. We can hunt him easily," he called out. The Wild People stopped dancing and leaped into their canoes.

These people had been fiercely protecting a secret. They had a summer garden. All the plants in the world were in that garden: tobacco, corn, squash, and potatoes.

But when the Wild People took off in their canoes, paddling to the island thinking the tree stump was a moose, water leaked into all of their canoes, and their paddles all snapped in two. This allowed the seven Micmac men to hurry across the lake in the darkness and find the garden.

The Micmacs opened their deer-hide pouches and gathered plants of each species before returning home across the meadow and mountains. Thanks to Muskrat Person and the gift from Skunk Woman, the seven were able to bring the plants back to the Micmac people so that they could all grow gardens and save food for winter.

The Weasel Sisters Marry the Star People

(Adapted from Six Worlds, Whitehead, p.162, and as told by Tomah Josephs)

Long ago, all of the stars had names. They were star-people, shape-changers. They could come down to earth if they choose. They still have names even now. There is a bear and the Bear's Den. Seven little stars together make up the Bear's Den. The red star is Robin. There are the Hunter stars with their fishing lines of stars. They are trying to catch Fish Hawk stars. Old Man Star is the North Star, He Who Seldom Blinks. The morning star is The Last One Made. Gluskape taught these names to the people. The stars are alive. And many people sang songs about them.

Passamaquoddy Poem, about 1850

We are the stars that sing.

We sing with out light.

We are the birds of fire.

We fly over the heavens.

Our light is a star.

One time, two Weasel Sisters climbed a tall tree, an oak. It was night, and Night Walker had come out. The two silly girls looked up at the star people. They talked about them and teased each other.

One said to the other, "Those stars are so close. Wouldn't you like to live in the sky and walk on soft clouds all day? Which would you take for a husband?"

"It would be the little red one. I like little stars best and he twinkles so brightly."

"Fine. Then I will choose the Great Yellow Star."

They joked a while longer and then fell asleep. However, making jokes at night before falling asleep can sometimes cause problems. Those jokes may come true. When those two Weasel Sisters awoke the next morning, they found out that they had been married, at their single word and were no longer living on the earth.

As the older weasel sister awoke, she heard a man saying, "Take care. This cloud is not big. You will knock over my war paints." She sat up and saw a tall, noble man lying next to her.

The second sister opened her eyes to find a little red-eyed man saying, "Be careful, or you will spill the water I need for the heat of my red eyes."

Then the Weasel Sisters burst into tears. "We were joking about marrying you! We didn't mean to come here. Look! There are no people here, no animals. Our parents won't know where we are!"

Star People are very kind. The two old men tried to comfort the girls with maple sugar, as you would comfort a crying baby.

"Many girls have to marry and leave their homes far behind. It's beautiful here; the stars sing night after night, The moon is close too. And we will take good care of you. Now dry your tears. You'll be happy here soon enough."

Yet, yellow, red, young, or old, none of the Star People could make the silly girls happy young wives. In a few days, these two Weasel Sisters grew tired of living in the star country, above the earth that they demanded to go home.

"Just stay a little longer," Yellow Star said. "But you mustn't leave without our help." And the Star People went hunting for the whole day.

And whenever they left the girls alone, they said, "You see that rock over there on that cloud? Do not lift that large stone no matter what."

The girls agreed at first. However, after a week of this, the younger sister, who was bored and homesick, rushed to the flat stone and lifted it up just a little. She gazed through the hole.

"Look! Sister, come here!" Below they saw the sky itself, clouds and rainbows.

Below that was the earth where they had lived, and she could see their childhood home, its woods and rivers. Then, with broken hearts, both girls began to weep.

The Star People are not harsh or evil. With their power, they knew at once that the Weasel sisters had peeked beneath the stone. When they returned that night, the Star husbands said that the girls could return home.

"But," Red Star warned, "It won't be easy to travel back the way you have come. So, listen carefully to what you must do."

"When you awake tomorrow," said Yellow Star, "Don't open your eyes. Wait until you hear the song of the chickadee. Stay quiet and listen a while longer. Next, you will hear the song of the red squirrel. Still you must keep your eyes closed and wait. Finally, you will hear the chipmunk sing. You must be patient. Then you may get up and look around."

The next morning, the sisters awoke eager to be home as soon as possible. The younger sister was especially eager. When she heard the chickadee sing, she wanted to jump up, but her sister stopped her.

"Did you forget? Wait until the chipmunk sings."

Soon they heard the red squirrel chattering and singing at his morning's work. On hearing that, both girls could wait no more and they opened their eyes as they jumped up. They instantly found themselves on earth, indeed, but they were on top of a very tall hemlock tree with no way to climb down. As the animals had sung each song, the girls would have been drawn closer and closer to the earth if they had been patient. Instead, they sat trapped, high in the tree on a bed of moss.

The day dawned. Many people walked by and the girls called out for help.

First, they called to Moose Person, Tiom. "Elder brother, please help us. If you help us down, we will marry you and help you."

He looked up and said scowling, "I was married last fall." Then went on his way.

Next, to pass by was Bear Person, Mooin. "Elder brother, please help us climb down. We will marry you."

"I was married last spring," he growled. He went on his way.

At last came Wolverine, or Lox, a deceitful one. He heard them cry out for help high in the tree. He stopped and considered perhaps there might be a way he could tease them or torment them later on. So, he agreed to help.

While he climbed the tree, the girls realized in shock who he was and hatched a scheme.

First, he brought down the younger sister. Then he climbed back again and brought down the second sister.

"Thank you," she said as she touched the ground, "but I forgot my hair string. Please can you bring it down, and for your trouble we will go and build you a bride's wigwam."

The Wolverine was pleased with the thought. So, Lox climbed the tree again.

While he was gone, the two girls quickly built a wigwam. In it, they placed thorns, burrs, briers, and prickles of all kinds. Then they brought in hornets, stinging flies, and ants. These tricky sisters were also friends with the Flint People.

It took Lox the Wolverine most of the day to untie the hair string.

Meanwhile, the girls made a bridal bed of hornet's nests, an ant's nest for a chair, and sharp flints covered the floor. Finally, Lox untied the string, climbed down, and wearily headed for the wigwam, thinking he'd find the girls inside and a warm meal waiting.

Instead, as he entered, he ran into the thorns, which pierced his nose. The Flints cut his paws so that he roared aloud and sat down hard on the anthill seat. The Ants bit him in the rear, and as he squealed with pain, he heard a voice saying, "Come to me. I am the younger sister."

He leaped off the chair and fell on the bed of hornets, and that was the worst of all! The girls laughed and laughed at his discomfort. Then they ran home to their family before he could recover. He was so furious with the Weasel Sisters for this trick that from that day on, Lox the Wolverine has been very bad tempered, and rushes through the woods in search of the Weasel Sisters and the hornets biting his nose.

Part 3

A Boy Named Fox Fire

(Nova Scotia, Newfoundland- 1925)

A long time ago, an old woman and man lived in a wigwam. Because they were old and had no son to help them, they were very poor and just managed to get by.

One day, the old woman was gathering pine bark for a fire. In the forest, she saw a log of foxfire, and she heard a noise come from inside the log. She thought that perhaps it was the voice of a ghost because the People left logs of foxfire near burial sites. Perhaps a ghost was lost. Perhaps that ghost had not made it to the spirit world and was hiding in the log.

The voice was crying. This poor ld woman had power. She wasn't afraid. Inside the log, she found a baby boy. She lifted him out and wiped the moss off him. She wrapped the baby in the pointed part of the hood of her robe, and took him home with her.

"I found a baby in the forest," she told her husband. "We should keep him."

"All right," he said. "But what should we feed him?"

Because she had power, the old woman knew how to take care of this child. "We will feed him moose brains," she said.

67

So, the old man went out and killed a moose. The old woman named the baby Foxfire and fed him moose brains until he was one year old. The old woman was very strong. She had much power. She could see ten days into the future. When the boy turned two, she began to train him, to give him power too.

One day, she caught a chipmunk and skinned it. She stretched and pounded the skin for a long time to make it extra soft. All the time she pounded it, she spoke to it, she sang to it.

"Chipmunk, do all I tell you for my son, Foxfire. Here is what you must do. Go ahead of him. See ahead of him. Tell him all you know."

She then gave the chipmunk skin to the boy. Years later, the people had to go to war. They wanted to bring Foxfire with them, to cook for them and see into the future for them because they needed to travel deep into enemy country. They were going deep into Kwetej [caribou} country and that tribe had the power to shape change into caribou.

They set out. Every morning, the warrior chief spoke to Foxfire.

"Have you dreamed anything? Do you see anything ahead of us?"

Every morning, the boy Foxfire told him there was no danger ahead.

Finally, a morning came when he said, "Today I will know something."

He took out his chipmunk skin and his medicine bag. He spoke to the skin, "I want you to go, go ahead of us. See what lies ahead. What dangers lie before us? Go!"

At that, the chipmunk skin filled with power and the skin took shape. It ran ahead and saw tomorrow and then it returned. The chipmunk crawled into the boy's robe. It crawled onto his shoulder and spoke into his ear.

"There is danger," the chipmunk spirit said. "This war chief will die. He will die in two days time."

The people reached the fighting place, a large mountain but flat and level on top. The war party stopped at the bottom of the mountain. Foxfire told the chief of the danger and how the chipmunk had warned that the chief's death was near.

"I'll go up the mountain first," said Foxfire. "I will dance the War Medicine Dance on the top."

So he did. He climbed the mountain and danced there. While he danced, the Kwetej began to shoot at him. They weren't using arrows, but they were using metal, lead musket balls from white people. It didn't matter. The lead balls were trapped by his robe and didn't pierce his body. He returned to the war chief.

"Older brother," said Foxfire, "There are many of them. And, they have weapons from the white men, muskets and their bows. They will surround us soon. You must go dance now."

When the war chief climbed the mountain, the Kwetej killed him as the Chipmunk had foretold. Foxfire didn't give up. He began to dream, hoping for power.

Then he said to the others, "The enemy is surrounding us, coming from behind. They are wearing caribou feet so that we won't see their footprints. Don't worry. They can't see us. By our power and preparations, we are invisible to them."

So it was that the Kwetej warriors passed around the war party and never saw them. Then Foxfire and the Micmacs took the caribou feet, and now that they have them, they can travel wherever they want, for caribou are great travelers.

Gluskape and Turtle Person

(Micmac, Nova Scotia, recorded in 1894)

In olden times, the chief of Pictou in Nova Scotia had three beautiful daughters. The youngest was the loveliest. When Turtle Person, Mikchick, saw her, he thought, "She is the one I want to marry." However, so did all the other young men around.

In their jealously, they agreed to kill anyone who dared try to win her. Turtle Person was neither handsome nor wealthy. He thought he had no chance to impress the chief and his daughter.

So, Turtle Person went to visit his nephew Gluskape and told him about his problem.

"Don't worry, Uncle. I'll help you," Gluskape said.

The next day, Gluskape went to the village with a handful of shiny wampum beads. He gave these to the chief and proposed marriage on behalf of Turtle Person. The wife of the chief agreed to the marriage proposal since Gluskape had asked him. So the youngest daughter went into her wigwam and made a bed of fresh twigs and soft pine boughs. She covered this bed with a white bear-skin. Then they brought Turtle Person to the wigwam and had dried meat for supper. So the two were married.

As the weeks went by, the girl worried. Turtle Person seemed very slow and lazy. While other young men hunted, he lounged by the fire and warmed himself. His young wife said to him, "You must hunt for us. If things go on this way, we will soon starve."

When he put on his snowshoes and went into the woods, the girl followed him. He hadn't gone far when the clumsy fellow tripped and fell down. The girl ran home and told her mother that he was worthless. Perhaps Gluskape had tricked them as he sometimes does.

"Turtle Person will do something yet. Be patient," her mother said.

One day, Gluskape came to the camp. He had foreseen something. He said to Turtle Person, "Tomorrow there will be a big game of ball. You must play, but because the young men are jealous of you, they will try to kill you during the fame by crowding you and trampling on you. It will happen near your father-in-law's lodge. To escape them, I will give you the power to jump high over the lodge. This you will do twice, but the third time, something bad will happen to you. I am sorry, but so it must be."

The next day, the young men began the ball game. Twice they tried to kill Turtle Person, but twice he escaped them by leaping over the lodge like a bird flying. Again, they chased him. On the third jump, he was stuck. He was caught on top of the ridgepoles and hung there dangling in the tobacco smoke that rose from below.

Now it was Gluskape, who sat in the lodge, smoking his pipe.

As Turtle Person hung there, he said, "Don't worry, Uncle, I will make you a sachem of all Turtles, and you will rise up a great nation. When I leave, this land may well be in your hands."

Turtle Person was alarmed. Gluskape was his nephew. "What do you mean you are going to leave?"

Gluskape laughed. "Never mind. Let's get you down from there."

This was how Gluskape covered Turtle Person with the sacred tobacco smoke. He smoked him so long that Turtle Person's skin became hard and shell-like, and the smokey patterns may still be seen there. Then Gluskape rose up and took out Turtle Person's entrails, leaving only one short one.

"Nephew, what are you doing to my insides? I will die!"

"No," said Gluskape. "I am giving you a great life. From this day on, you may roll through fire and never feel it, and you can live on both land and water."

So, Turtle Person rejoiced. All these gifts of m'teouin came none too soon. For the next day, the young men went on a hunt, and Gluskape warned that again, they would try to kill him.

The young men rushed ahead through the forest, but Turtle Person followed slowly behind. At least so they thought. For with his new power, he flew through the air and killed a moose deep in the woods. He dragged the big moose out to the snowshoe track and opened his pouch of tobacco and pipe. When his enemies arrived, he was sitting on the moose carcass, smoking.

This angered the men more than ever. Yet, they did nothing. This slow, clumsy fellow had leapt over the lodge, been smoked and roasted by fire and now he killed a moose? They returned to camp arguing among themselves.

Now, it was summer and Gluskape was planning a trip away from Pictou. He came to the camp to say goodbye and to talk to Turtle Person.

"The young men will build a big fire and throw you in it. Nevertheless, go cheerfully. For my power will keep you safe. After that, they will try to drown you, and you must beg that they not do it."

Turtle Person agreed. "Goodbye, Gluskape. Good journey. Let us meet again," he said cheerfully.

The next day, the fire was built. The men grabbed Turtle Person and threw him into it. He simply rolled over, went to sleep since he was such a lazy fellow, and liked a good, warm nap. When the fire burned low, he woke up.

"Hey, bring me more wood. The fire is out and I'm cold," he called.

73

"No. No more wood. Let's drown him!" the young men cried. Angrily, the men seized him. "Take him to the lake!"

"Oh, please don't. Put me back in the fire," begged Turtle Person. "Don't throw me in the water. Anything but that."

"Ha, ha. Finally, he's scared. We will throw you deep into the lake, and that will be the end of you!"

They dragged Turtle Person through the woods. He screamed, yelled and clawed at them. He tore up trees, rocks and roots. They dragged him along as if he were a madman. They put him in a canoe and paddled out into the middle of the lake. They tossed him overboard. Down into the dark, dark water Turtle Person sank. They watched as he vanished below like a stone. Satisfied, they returned to camp.

The next day was hot and sunny. Around noontime, something could be seen basking on a large rock about mile out in the middle of the lake. Two men took a canoe and paddled quickly out to investigate. There lay Turtle Person, sunning himself on the rock. As they reached out to seize him, he smiled at them and said, "Goodbye."

He rolled over, kerplump, into the water, where he is living happily with his wife and children to this day. And, this is why all turtles ever since that early time tip-tilt themselves into the water whenever they see anyone coming.

The Orphan and the Mikumwess

(Micmac. Rand, 1894)

In the olden times, there was a large camp of the people. One of the people was an orphan, a young man. He lived with his grandmother and hunted with the other young men. Because he was ugly and clumsy, people often laughed at him. He was slow. When they hunted, he often fell behind. One time, when he lagged behind, a big storm came. The wind was blowing hard and the rain poured down. Soon he was completely lost.

He grew colder and colder and was ready to give up and die, when he saw something. It was a man.

The man smiled. "You're lost. Why don't you come home with me and I'll give you something to eat. You can dry your clothes by my fire."

They went to the man's wigwam. It was filled with smoked meat, cakes of fat, and bags of marrow. It was full of the furs of otter, moose, mink, beaver, and muskrat. The furs were stuffed behind the lodge poles all around. The boy had never seen such wealth. The stranger fed him food and drink. They smoked tobacco and talked. Finally, they fell asleep.

In the morning, the man gave the ugly boy many presents to take home. He piled the boy high with furs and meat. The pack got so heavy that the young man couldn't lift it onto his back.

"Don't worry," said the man. "I'll come with you and carry this."

He lifted the pack easily and off they went, walking until they could see the camp of the people in the distance.

"I can't go any further," said the man. "But if you should ever need me, come to this spot and I'll find you." Then he left.

The orphan walked into his camp, eager to tell his grandmother that he had returned with meat. When the people ran out to greet him, he learned that he had been missing in the woods for one year. Everyone thought he had drowned or starved. Then the orphan knew he had been with Mikumwess, one of the little people who live in the forest.

He told no one. Instead, he said, "I have been hunting. My pack is back there."

The people helped him carry in the big load of meat and skins. Not one man could lift it, so they had to break it into small loads.

One night, he said to his grandmother, "You should go and make an evening visit to the chief."

His grandmother knew then that he wanted to take a wife. Therefore, she went to the chief's wigwam and entered.

"Sagamore, my grandson and I are tired of living alone. I am old and feeble and need help." That was all she said, but the chief knew she wanted to ask for his daughter in marriage.

"No. your grandson is ugly and lazy. You are poor. I cannot help you with your problem."

So, the old woman went home and told the orphan what had happened. He didn't grow angry. He merely said, "We can't do anything about this. It is not our fault."

In the morning, he returned to the spot where the Mikumwess had left him. The Mikumwess was there smiling at him again. They walked away together and they killed a big moose. They butchered it and cut it in half. The Mikumwess lifted his half onto his back. He said to the young man, "Go ahead. Pick up the moose."

To his amazement, he lifted the moose onto his shoulders. That evening, Mikumwess took out an alder-wood flute. He played and made beautiful sounds, like birds singing, like whales singing.

"Here," he said to the young man. "Play, I'll show you."

He taught the orphan, who was delighted to play this music. He stayed two nights, playing and playing on the alder flute. When he prepared to leave, the Mikumwess gave him presents again.

Already he had given him strength and music. Now, he took away the young man's ugliness and turned him into a handsome Mikumwess with their magic power.

The orphan returned home, carrying another huge load of meat and furs.
He strode into camp with the load. Everyone was amazed to see him and he learned that he had been gone for two years. In the evening, he brought out his flute and began to

play. The beautiful sound floated throughout the camp. All the young women hurried into their wigwams, dressed in their finery, and painted pretty designs on their faces. The girls walked by the young man's wigwam, hoping he would notice them. They entered his wigwam, but he turned his back and wouldn't look at them.

Finally, he spoke. "We have no need to trouble you or even to think of you." And, they left.

A week passed. "Grandmother, I want you to make an evening visit," he said.

"Where shall I go this time?"

"Go to the poor wigwam on the other side of the camp. Those two girls have no mother or father. They live alone. Go there."

The grandmother went to the little wigwam. She entered and sat by the fire. She said to one, "Will you come live with us?"

The orphan girl was quiet and polite. She said, "If you and your grandson both wish it, I'll come."

"Good. This will be a good thing for all of us."

The girl went with her that very night. Later, her sister came too. Then to get away from the jealously of that camp of people, they all moved deep into the forest and lived there very well.

The Girl Who Married Katahdin

(Penobscot, told by Marie Saksis)

In olden times, a girl was gathering blueberries on the slopes of the great
mountain, Kahtahdin. As she wandered about, filling her basket, she felt lonely.

"How I wish I had a husband," she said to herself.

She looked up and saw the great mountain, rising up before her in all its glory,
with the red, gleaming sunlight on the peak, and she added, "I wish that Katahdin were a
man, and that he would marry me."

Then she went on gathering blueberries. Some storm clouds blew up and
gathered deep purple behind the mountain. She heard a rumbling of the earth and a
scattering of boulders rattled down the cliffs. Out of the woods, stepped a handsome
young man. His face was stern and his eyebrows gray and fierce, but she was not afraid
of him.

She greeted him and he led her into a cave that had appeared in the side of the
mountain. Then the mountainside closed behind them and she found herself in a huge
cavern where the young man of the mountain lived.

Meanwhile, in the camp, her parents wondered where she had gone. They
searched for her and found the basket of berries, but there were no bear tracks, no tracks

79

of enemy warriors, nothing to explain where she had gone and what had happened.

For three years, the girl lived inside the mountain. In time, she gave birth to a baby boy, but she was all by herself there with just the baby, and she grew lonely for her family.

One day, she begged her husband, "Please let me go home and see my family. I must show them their grandson. I beg you."

So he agreed. "Go in peace," he said. "But never tell anyone who has married you."

She took the baby and climbed down the mountain, walking for several days, until she rejoined her family. They exclaimed over the beauty of the baby, but his little eyebrows were made of stone and this puzzled them. They began to wonder if somehow the Great Spirit of the Mountain had taken the girl for his wife.

The little boy grew. He had strange and unusual gifts. When he pointed his finger at a moose, it would drop dead. When out in the canoe on the lake, when he pointed at a flock of wild ducks, or wild swans flying overhead, then the lake was covered at once with floating game. The men could then lean over the edge of the canoe and gather up the birds. So, because of the boy, his mother and the tribe had enough to eat.

Now, the Great Spirit Katahdin had married this girl thinking that the boy would one day build a strong nation and make the Wabanaki a mighty tribe, as was the Algonquin. He had warned the girl, "Do not answer questions about who the boy's father is. The tribe's people should know it themselves by seeing him and his powers. They should not trouble you with curious and impertinent questions of how we were married."

However, the tribe's people were curious about the boy, and they asked the young woman, "Who is his father?"

She said, "I have brought you all that you need. Please show me respect. Don't ask me such questions. See for yourself how it is."

But, the people were endlessly curious. They gossiped among themselves about what had happened during those three years that she had been gone. They didn't even try to restrain themselves from asking her again and again where she had been, where the boy had come from. They teased her and tormented her. They spoke to her without dignity or respect, insulting her and the little boy.

Finally, their ceaseless nagging infuriated her. She thought to herself, "Truly Katahdin was right. These people are not worthy of my son, nor shall he serve them. He shall not lead them to great victories. They don't have the character to create a great nation."

She said aloud, "You fools! By your own folly, you will kill yourselves. You mud wasps! You sting the fingers of the one who would pluck you from the water. Why do you trouble me constantly to tell you what you should know already? Look at what I have brought you! Can't you see who the father of my boy is? Behold his stony eyebrows. Do you not know Katahdin by them? Now it is too late. You have brought great sorrow on yourselves by your endless teasing. From this day forward, you may find your own food; find your own deer and moose. This child and his powers will not help you anymore."

The young woman took the hand of her little son. Together they walked into the woods and up the side of the great mountain. They were never seen again.

Dusk

(There are many stories of Gluskape leaving and Wabanaki searching for him. Some say he went to live deep in the great mountain Katahdin and some say he paddled far to the east past Newfoundland.)

Gluskape had freed the Dawnland from all the ice giants, cannibal giants, the huge walls of ice. He had conquered the Chenoos, who covered themselves with pinesap and rolled on the ground until they were covered with leaves and branches. He had stopped the flooding of the rivers and had quieted the Kulloo, the giant wind-bird. He had taught the Wabanaki people many things- how to make tools, how to catch whales, how to behave with respect, to avoid gossip and jealously.

There came a time when the people, although they worshiped him, they were not grateful or kind. They indulged in vicious gossip and were often quarrelsome and jealous. This enraged Gluskape. They ignored what he told them to be kind and share whatever they had. The animals turned away from the People as well, and they no longer spoke the same language.

Finally, Gluskape decided to leave. He gave a lavish feast and invited all the animals – Turtle Person, Marten, Woodchuck, Moose, Loon –they all came. At the end of the feast, Gluskape got into a great canoe. The animals gathered on the shore and he pushed off to sea.

They stood and watched as the Master of the Dawnland paddled farther and farther away to the east. They watched until they could see him no more. They could still hear his voice, singing, further and further in the distance, fainter and fainter.

When the sound of his singing died away, a great silence fell on all the Dawnland. The animals, who until now had spoken one language together with the people, could no longer understand each other, and they each ran off in their own way. Never since have they met in council in friendship or in peace.

All of Nature in the Dawnland mourned the passing of Gluskape. The great Snowy Owl fled deep into the forest where he sings this sad song – Koo-koo-kooos, which means, "I am sorry. I am sorry."

The loons, Kwimu, who had so loyally hunted and kept company with Gluskape, searched restlessly up and down the lakes and rivers, calling mournfully for their master.

New people were arriving in the Dawnland, with guns and axes.

There are some stories of these tall wooden ships, the white sails, the metal bullets, and terrible diseases. There is even a tale of Gluskape sailing to Europe in one of these sailing ships and persuading the British royalty to stop colonizing his land.

There are stories of the Anglo settlers taking over the huge Dawnland forests, creating total disharmony for the animals, plants, and people – who had existed here for the previous 12,000 years. In this way, the m'teouin, the power of Gluskape, was slowly lost.

Micmac Poem Today
By Red Hawk, on the power of stones – 1983

The forest sings itself into darkness

And, the stone holds a light

He can feel in his palm;

It is the same light animals leave

On the stones along the river

Where they have passed in the night.

Do we think of the stones we walk on? Do we feel the power of the clouds and wonder when the first winds blew? Do we sit quietly when worried, waiting to feel the power in the natural world around us before making a decision, each seeking to find our own way, a way that will help others and show respect for the earth? Do we envy those who have more than we do and hope that things will go badly for them?

I hope that through coming to know these stories, we can take a step closer to knowing the true history of a land we all now share with the Wabanaki, animals, and plants of northeast North America. Perhaps, someday, we will learn to treat nature and other cultures with more sensitivity and respect, as Gluskape taught 12,000 years ago.

These tales now, as always, remain the cultural property of the four Wabinaki tribes. So, WOLIWONI! Thank you for reading them with respect.

www.ingramcontent.com/pod-product-compliance
Lightning Source LLC
Chambersburg PA
CBHW071825020426
42331CB00007B/1612